Presented

To:

_____

On this special occasion by:

_____

My name is:

_____

Also by Ernst Saint-Louis

Dying To Save Others
Jesus, The Great Healer
La Joie d'Aimer les Autres
Jésus, le Grand Guérisseur
El Gozo De Amar Los Otros
Jesús, el gran Médico

Through Worship Only

ERNST SAINT-LOUIS

WESTBOW
P R E S S®
A DIVISION OF THOMAS NELSON
& ZONDERVAN

Photos credits: Istock; WikipediA;
Eric J. Saint-Louis
Editing credits: Jessie Saint-Louis

Scripture taken from the King James Version of the Bible.

Scripture quotations marked (NIV) are taken from the Holy Bible, New
International Version®, NIV®. Copyright © 1973, 1978, 1984, 2011 by Biblica,
Inc.™ Used by permission of Zondervan. All rights reserved worldwide. www.
zondervan.com The "NIV" and "New International Version" are trademarks
registered in the United States Patent and Trademark Office by Biblica, Inc.™

Scripture taken from the New King James Version®. Copyright © 1982
by Thomas Nelson. Used by permission. All rights reserved.

WestBow Press books may be ordered through booksellers or by contacting:

WestBow Press
A Division of Thomas Nelson & Zondervan
1663 Liberty Drive
Bloomington, IN 47403
www.westbowpress.com
1 (866) 928-1240

ISBN: 978-1-5127-9638-4 (sc)
ISBN: 978-1-5127-9639-1 (hc)
ISBN: 978-1-5127-9637-7 (e)

Library of Congress Control Number: 2017911275

Print information available on the last page.

WestBow Press rev. date: 02/28/2018

It IS " *THROUGH* *WORSHIP* *ONLY*" we can mingle

joyfully with the Lord of lords. Isn't why king David

longed to live in God's house all his life? Shouldn't it

be the same for us, too? If not where else should

we dwell in holiness and happiness with our Maker!

"The one thing I ask of the LORD—
the thing I seek most—
is to live in the house of the LORD all the days of my life,
delighting in the LORD's perfections
and meditating in his Temple."

I am grateful to my Lord for He has blessed

me with a great message.

Indeed, Father God has lifted me up!

A personal and powerful revelation that the author didn't anticipate. However, God chooses for reasons known only to Him.

Contents

"Through Worship Only"—The essence of what this book is all about. Those are not my own words. They are the words from the sky.

I hope that each reader understands the importance of true worship. We need to take this very seriously for God wants all the glory. Therefore, we are not supposed to be the center for ***Soli Deo gloria*—Glory to God alone.**

Are we in for idolatry worship or true worship?

"I, John, am the one who heard and saw these things.
And when I had heard and seen them, I fell down to worship
at the feet of the angel who had been showing them to me.
But he said to me, don't do that! I am a fellow
servant with you and with your fellow prophets and with
all who keep the words of this scroll. **Worship God!"**
Revelation 22:8, 9 (NIV)

I enter not into the paths of the wicked. I enter not in the way of evil men. But I enter into your path, dear Lord, into your Holy Hill to exalt and to praise Emmanuel, my Savior, where I can meet your holiness –

Through Worship Only

For in your presence is abundant joy and profound peace!

Introduction

This book is the result of a personal revelation from heaven. Made and called to worship the Creator in the beauty and the splendor of His holiness; here we are to acknowledge His majesty. Worship is recognizing our dependence upon Him. Must we avow today's worship is full of all types of negative human emotions and feel-good sensations in the flesh; instead of the true worship that our Creator deserves and expects from His creatures. Men act like spectators; but Father God is the only spectator and we are supposed to be the actors. We forget we are worshipers. And we are supposedly worshipping Father God, not ourselves. Ethan Beh, author of the book *Never Lose Control Again* wrote, "There is a huge list of human emotions that we are capable of experiencing. However, oftentimes we only experience a very limited number of positive emotions."

Indeed, when we gather to worship we may have failed to experience the positive emotions as we should have and missed many blessings Father God is anxious to give us. Unfortunately, we experienced the negative ones when we meet to worship. Of the list, we found that the very first concern is to show off and feel good about ourselves. Then we start to worry if we are not allowed to do just that, and we are automatically frustrated, angry, unhappy, and become distressed.

And for some, worship day becomes a thorny predicament instead of taking the delight in the Lord and His day of worship. While we are supposed to come to worship the Most High with humbleness, reverence, thanksgiving, and gratefulness to make worship day very exciting, joyful, and delightful, in the place we are worshipping ourselves. For Apostle Paul, a sinful mind is hostile to

Father God. "Those controlled by the sinful nature cannot please God," Romans 8:8 (NIV). Remember negative emotions are the results of sin. Beware, for true worship is a matter of heart.

We should not come in God's presence with boastfulness, arrogance, hatred, jealousy, and envy; but with trust, confidence, contentment, enthusiasm, affection, forgiveness, gratitude and love. True worshippers make worship day a day of rejoicing and happiness. A day of celebration for God's compassion, His forgiveness, His love, His goodness, and His faithfulness, and the beauty of His holiness, which continues through all generations. Worship day is a day of praise, of healing, of excitement, of victory over sin, and love for one another. All worshippers should sing and shout joyfully to the Almighty who is among us. It is also a day of forgiveness. "Therefore, if you are presenting your offering at the altar, and there you remember that your brother has done something against you, leave your offering there before the altar and go; first be reconciled with your brother, and then come and present your offering," as stated in Matthew 5:23,24 (NIV). Jesus added: "For I was hungry and you gave me something to eat, I was thirsty and you gave me something to drink, I was a stranger and you invited me in, I needed clothes and you clothed me, I was sick and you looked after me, I was in prison and you came to visit me," Matthew 25:35,36 (NIV).

That is true worship, according to Jesus. Furthermore, *God's Word came through the prophet Micah*: "He hath shewed thee, O man, what is good; and what doth the LORD require of thee, but to do justly, and to love mercy, and to walk humbly with thy God?" Micah 6:8 (KJV). Indeed, we are made and called to worship the good Lord who made the heavens, the earth, the sea and the springs of water, not just one day but every day of the week!

All humankind is called to worship and to obey the Maker, the great King above all gods, faithfully, loyally, and joyfully. Therefore, the Bible invites us all: "O come, let us sing unto the LORD: let us make a joyful noise to the rock of our salvation. Let us come before his presence with thanksgiving, and make a joyful noise unto him with psalms. For the LORD is a great God, and a great King above all gods. In his hand are the deep places of the earth: the strength of the hills is his also. The sea is his, and he made it: and his hands formed the dry land. O come, let us worship and bow down: let us kneel before the LORD our maker. For he is our God; and we are the people of his pasture, and the sheep of his hand."

Psalm 95:1-7 (KJV)

"And when the wise men from the East had come into the house, they saw the young Child with Mary His mother, and fell down and worshiped Him," Matthew 2:11 (NKJV).

We enter to worship the Lord of lords
For He brought us forth from our mother's womb!
For the earth is full with His goodness!
For the wonderful works He had made!
For His great blessings we are enjoying on a daily basis!

1

Worshipping God

"Their land is full of idols; they bow down to the work of their hands, to what their fingers have made." Isaiah 2:8 (NIV)

"The loftiness of man shall be bowed down,
And the haughtiness of men shall be brought low;
The LORD alone will be exalted in that day,
But the idols He shall utterly abolish,"
Isaiah 2:17,18 (NKJV).

Worship

is an interaction between the worshipper and God. It started with Abel, Seth, Enosh, Noah, Abraham, and Moses who "bowed to the ground at once and worshipped Yahweh." Genesis 4: 26 and Exodus 34:8 (NIV). The other inhabitants worshipped things that God had made, such as the sun, the moon, and the stars. Later on they worshipped rivers, hills, and mountains. They also made images of stone and wood, which they worshipped and called the images of gods. But Abel, Seth, Enosh, Noah, Abraham, and Moses worshipped God, the Creator of heaven and earth, the true and the living God. In fact, the tragedy in the story of Cain and Abel lies in the difference between true and false adoration. The first and greatest commandment is this: "You shall worship no other gods," Exodus 20:3 (NIV).

This book is an afflatus – a divine communication of knowledge. It is structured and centered on worship – around glorifying and praising God, the Almighty Father, our Creator and Savior who requires and deserves to be worshipped "in spirit and truth." John 4:24 (NKJV)

Let us define worship: according to Dr. Michael Morrison, "Although, the Bible doesn't give a formal definition of worship we can look at some: worship means "worth," and *scipe* or *ship,* which means for example, the English word "worship" comes from two Old English words: *weorth,* which means something like shape or "quality." Also the Old English word–*ship* in modern words like friend*ship* – represents the quality of being a friend. So worth-ship is the quality of having worth or of being worthy.

When we worship, we are saying that God has worth for all the marvelous things He has done.

He is worth adoring with reverence and celebration for His attributes. We listen to His words. We speak, we testify, we sing, and we witness Him for His goodness and His power. We were called to existence for the purpose of glorifying the Creator, praising Him, and worshipping Him. Notice in both Hebrew and Greek, there are two major kinds of descriptions for worship: 1) It is an act of respect and submission to bow down, to kneel, and to put one's face down. With body language, you are conveying the message. I will do your will, dear Lord. I am willing to obey. 2) It is a call to worship and to be holy, to be saved, to share God's love and to serve." The Bible clearly states that worship is the main purpose for which we are called as a chosen people so we do not walk in darkness but to be the light of the world. "You are a chosen people, a royal priesthood, a holy nation, a people belonging to God, that you may declare the praises of him who called you out of darkness into his wonderful light." 1 Peter 2:9 (NIV)

This book is written about glorifying Father God every single day and especially on worship day, which is the day of rest according to His instruction as we read in Genesis 2:1-3 (NIV):

"Thus the heavens and the earth were completed in their entire vast array in six days. By the seventh day God has finished the work he had been doing; and on this seventh day he rested from all His work. God blessed the seventh day and made it holy." We ought to live in faithfulness to God in every detail and in every aspect of life. Human emotions play a momentous role in our basic existence. Therefore, we cannot and should not ignore emotions when worshipping God and in our relationship with Him. We should put them in the proper place and value emotions when it comes to our spiritual life. Indeed, negative or positive emotions play a vital role in our physical and spiritual life. They cannot be overlooked in our intimate relation with Father God. With *Through Worship Only...* I am hoping that you get out of the paradigm you're stuck in when it comes to worship of Father God, the Creator "*in spirit and truth.*" John 4:24 (KJV). In this book, I am attempting to explain that Christ asks all true worshippers to go beyond merely keeping a day of worship.

I believe true worship to be a moment of forgiveness, repentance, thankfulness, rejoicing, happiness, enjoyment, and celebration. Managing our negative emotions, our hatred, our bitterness, our resentment, and the unforgiveness is not an option but a must for true worshipper. In fact, worship day is not a day of sorrowfulness, hostility, grief, despair, unhappiness, or lamentation. Supposedly we ought not to abandon our assembly according to the book of Hebrews 10:25 (NIV) : "not giving up meeting together, as some are in the habit of doing, but encouraging one another—and all the more as you see the day approaching." The assembly is a worship place where God is in the midst of His people who gather to render religious reverence and humble homage to Him, only to the Creator – *through worship only.*

Worship is a brotherly relationship with one another and with God, the Creator. Worship is not religious entertainment. It is a very serious matter for God. True worship preparation starts the first day of the week and Matthew 5 : 16 (NIV) says it well, "In the same way, let your light shine before others, that they may see your good deeds and glorify your Father in heaven."

Indeed, we worship because the great universe is created by the Most High God. For that He deserves to be worshipped. The Creator, our Father decided to create us because His main purpose was for us to worship on a daily basis – for we were made to worship Him anyway.

The main purpose of this book is to emphasize the importance of true worship – to worship as Christ worshiped. In this world of sadness, grief, and confusion, there has not been a timelier moment for us to worship the Almighty *in truth* It is the only way to stay in communion with God daily – *through worship only.* Worship is trusting Father God, seek Him and obey Him.

Let us come before Him with joyful songs and worship Him with gladness. For God-oriented people worship Him in truth while mammon-oriented people worship Him not. The reason that the Church (Body of Christ) is not powerful is simply because we failed to worship Father God personally and congregationally as He expects of us. So unfortunately, worship does not bring the most joy, power, and blessings as it is intended to be. (See Acts 2).

The love of power and to be worshipped

The devil artfully set the place back in the Garden of Eden with pitfalls, distractions, and brainwashing. The unscrupulous ruse Satan used to seduce Eve in the Garden is no different than what he is using today to deceive us. Today the devil's agents are busy trying to imitate him cunningly. All for the love of power, money, fame, and glory. Above all, to worship Satan instead of worshiping the real Creator in spirit and truth like He requested.

As I am reflecting on the way many are worshipping the Creator today, it is obvious that Father God is not exalted but men are. And the prophet Isaiah continued, "The LORD alone will be exalted in that day, and the idols will totally disappear. People will flee to caves in the rocks and to holes in the ground from the fearful presence of the LORD and the splendor of his majesty, when he rises to shake the earth. In that day people will throw away to the moles and bats their idols of silver and idols of gold, which they made to worship. They will flee to caverns in the rocks and to the overhanging crags from the fearful presence of the LORD and the splendor of his majesty, when he rises to shake the earth," Isaiah 2:18-21 (NIV).

Deeper relationship with God

Far too many of us (or so called-Christians) do not give Father God the worship He deserves and we are not blessed after worship because blessings come from only true worship. We failed to offer worship that pleases Him. In his letter to the Corinthians, Paul wrote: "As the secrets of their hearts are laid bare. So they will fall down and worship God, exclaiming, God is really among you!"1 Corinthians 14:25 (NIV)

These days we witness so much personal recognition and so much personal expressions on the pulpit and we wonder if God is really in this. Many of us are engaging in activities that dishonor God, such as taking care of personal business in a deceitful way, showing off our pride, and honoring man and woman in the sacred hour of worshipping the holy God, on the pulpit.

It seems that they do not have to feel bad at all that they have hurt their conscience by lying about the word of God. Besides, when one desires is to hate or disobey the word, can we call that worship? When one comes to church to fight another, to curse another, with the intent to hurt others, to play politics as if the brethren are operating in the secular world, is that worship? Prophet Isaiah is even stronger – saying, in effect, in Isaiah 1:11-15 (NIV): "I have no pleasure in the blood of bulls and lambs and goats.... Stop bringing meaningless offerings! Your incense is detestable to me. New Moons, Sabbaths and convocations — I cannot bear your evil assemblies. Your New Moon festivals and your appointed feasts my soul hates... When you spread out your hands in prayer, I will hide my eyes from you; even if you offer many prayers, I will not listen." The people were doing rituals, bringing animals, keeping Sabbaths and festivals, even praying, but despite all that, there was something seriously *lacking* in their worship. Why didn't God like their worship? Well, some people are just not qualified to worship Father God. Simply put, their lives were full of sin; full of every kind of wickedness, anger, rage, lie, hate, envy, greed, and filled with all forms of malice, and evil.

So do we, and prophet Isaiah counsels. "Your hands are full of blood; wash and make yourselves clean... Stop doing wrong, learn to do right! Seek justice, encourage the oppressed. Defend the cause of the fatherless, plead the case of the widow," Isaiah 1:15-17 (NIV).

The same is true here as many of us didn't obey God's commands and our actions are not pleasing to God. We are not dealing with others as He asked us to do. When we disobey God's commands at home, at work, in our neighborhood, or in our relation with others, our worship is not acceptable. Our worship offering is given in vain. In Matthew 5:22-24 (NIV): "Jesus began to teach the crowds and said: But I tell you that anyone who is angry with a brother or sister will be subject to judgment. Again, anyone who says to a brother or sister, 'Raca,' is answerable to the court. And anyone who says, 'You fool!' will be in danger of the fire of hell. Therefore, if you are offering your gift at the altar and there remember that your brother or sister has something against you, leave your gift there in front of the altar. First go and be reconciled to them; then come and offer your gift."

When we come to worship empty, we leave empty because we adored in vain. When so many leaders (yes, even the so-called church leaders) are too partial toward others, is that worship? How can you practice partiality in your church activities when the God you are serving is impartial? In His Sermon on the Mount, "Jesus began to teach the crowds: If you love those who love you, what reward will you get? Are not even the tax collectors doing that? And if you greet only your own people, what are you doing more than others? Do not even pagans do that? Be perfect, therefore, as your heavenly Father is perfect." Matthew 5:46-48 (NIV). How can you visit certain members and despise others. Is that worship? Do you worship one day a week or every day of the week? Oh! What a reassurance and great comfort to know that Father God doesn't like *favoritism*. As Apostle Peter said in Acts 10:34 (NIV): "I now realize how true it is that God does not show favoritism." Isn't it why Jesus rebukes in many instances the Pharisees and the Scribes in Matthew 7 for their hypocrisy and their fake worships? Thus, the word of God can be nullified for the sake of improper tradition. There are hypocrites with all the human reasoning and logic available who are actually as dumb as sheep. Prophet Isaiah was right when he prophesized about this: "The Lord says: these people come near to me with their mouth and honor me with their lips, but their hearts are far from me. Their worship of me is based on merely human rules they have been taught" Isaiah 29:13 (NIV). Beware false worship.

Beware, therefore; we need to understand that not all kinds of worship are acceptable to the Creator because He is true and holy. Simply said: live to please Father God is true worship.

Today, many people worship all kinds of foolish things. Just like the teachers of law said to Jesus that they love God, their disobedience proved that they were in fact far from telling the truth. Their injustice, disobedience, and adherence to man's tradition instead of God's commandments proved the contrary. Isn't this the same for many of us?

Our love for God should give us the desire to obey Him if we are sincere, humble and true. Satan moves the authorities of this world to defy God's law and to gain control of man's mind by enforcing human laws. In his interaction with the church of Corinth, Apostle Paul stresses the importance for them to be wise in 1 Corinthians 3:18 (NIV): "Do not deceive yourselves. If any of you think you are wise by the standards of this age, you should become 'fool' so that you may become wise."

The Psalmist added: "Don't be fools or senseless because "senseless people do not know, fools do not understand," Psalm 92:6 (NIV). Take heed, and watch; the world is disobeying God with all kinds of winds of doctrine as lawmakers speak with confidence— we can do everything we like or want and we still serve and worship God and we still love God— but this is rubbish!

In this way, we worship Him in vain. The misunderstanding of the Pharisees and others was the main reason they confronted Jesus about so–called law, which was in fact the tradition of men. He never changes His law (The Ten Commandments) as many preached. His teaching towards the law is that we should obey it and our lives should reflect the teachings because He came to "fulfill" the law, never to abolish it: "Do not think that I have come to abolish the Law or the Prophets; I have not come to abolish them but to fulfill them," Matthew 5:17 (NIV).

A list of human emotions

When worshipping, there is a list of positive emotions we can experience. Unfortunately the list of emotions we've experienced from the positive side is short. We have experienced far too many negative emotions for our own curse. Oftentimes the prayers and, the songs are full of frustration, selfishness, pettiness, self-righteousness, pride, jealousy, revenge, envy, hostility, sadness, "power hungry", nervousness, greed, ungratefulness, anger, manipulation, rudeness, hatred, suspicions, and doubt, and we are drained. More and more often, some preachers are not really trying hard enough to help the worshippers meet God when delivering the word. And they fail to explain the worshipers that positive emotions can nourish them.

The world must be prepared to accept the consequence of disobeying Father God, according to Psalm 149 (NIV): "May the praise of God be in their mouths and a double-edged sword in their hands, to inflict vengeance on the nations and punishment on the peoples, to bind their kings with fetters, their nobles with shackles of iron, to carry out the sentence written against them — this is the glory of all his faithful people. Praise the LORD." Do we love God? Can we love God without loving our brethren, or is it impossible?

Recently I was having a conversation with a young Christian lady and I told her the title of one of my books, *The Joy of Loving Others* and she replied "It is very tough, Pastor to love difficult people." It is very tough indeed but with God's grace we can. Yes, we can because Jesus says so. Well, there is no way out so we ought to love one another. We can't love God and mistreat other people. Beware the false teachers because as long as we live in this world the enemy is trying his best to have us under his wings. This world belongs to the devil and we must carefully search the word of God for accuracy, for wisdom, for humility, and true worship. As the U.S. essayist, poet, and philosopher Ralph Waldo Emmerson delivered before the senior class in Divinity College, Cambridge, Massachusetts, "Whenever the pulpit is usurped by a formalist, then is the worshipper defrauded and disconsolate."

Only from true and real fellowship we are going to see God, and feel His presence. Remember what happened when the disciples were praying in the upper room. Was it real and true worship? Oh! Yes, real worship took place not fake adoration. True worship took place because they were abiding in Christ. Again they were united in love for one another and joined together constantly in prayer, along with the women and Mary, the mother of Jesus, and with His brothers. In addition, we read in Acts 2:1-4 (NIV): "When the day of Pentecost came, they were all together in one place. Suddenly a sound like the blowing of a violent wind came from heaven and filled the whole house where they were sitting. They saw what seemed to be tongues of fire that separated and came to rest on each of them. All of them were filled with the Holy Spirit and began to speak in other tongue as the Spirit enabled them."

Worship in hatred is a no-no for true worshippers. Worship in jealousy, and envy damage your relationship with Father God. We are ashamed to recognize that we are responsible for all these unfortunate events because we do not give God a chance to rule over our hearts. It is very clear that many ignore and don't like God's rule. They hate God's reign over them. Just like the evolutionist scientists, they wanted to disqualify the Creator of all things by promoting the "theory of evolution."

There is no question that we need to be obedient, but whom you obey clearly shows who is ruling over you. We make the Lord God and His kingdom a priority in our life by loving and caring for one another. Loving His kingdom above the world and experiencing His grace is to know Him personally, not just adhering to His message of love, but loving Him above all. Loving your neighbors as yourself is part of God's loving package, which is why if you hate your neighbor, you also hate God. This is also part of worshipping Him.

All of us need to have or express positive feelings of profound adoration for our great God: a sacred personage. Therefore, we have to render homage and reverence to Him.

To celebrate His great name with praise and prayer, thanksgiving, shouting and singing loudly with joy and loving others, caring for others and giving ourselves so others can live as the Psalmist puts it in Psalm 42:4 (NIV): "These things I remember as I pour out my soul: how I used to go to the house of God under the protection of the Mighty One with shouts of joy and praise among the festive throng."

And the Psalmist further added: "Yet the LORD will command his lovingkindness in the daytime, and in the night his song shall be with me, and my prayer unto the God of my life," Psalm 42: 8 (KJV). Thank God for His wisdom and His intervention to break the alliance of Satan and man against heaven, which sets man free when he accepts the righteousness of Jesus Christ.

I strongly encourage you all to take seriously the biblical warnings that come from God. Unfortunately, many do not heed His warnings.

We should adore Him because He fills us with hope!

He provides us the best wheat!

He can always be trusted!

If He had not been merciful we would have been destroyed!

His kindness never fails!

So we bow to worship the King of kings, the Creator and the Almighty!

For the wonderful works He had made and all of the above… reverent honor and homage to the Highest for He merits excessive adoration!

For the wonderful works He had done and as expected all His wonders still work precisely and faithfully. Above all we are a product of God's workmanship. Therefore, the Creator owns us and we owe Him adoration!

As Apostle Paul encourages the Romans to present their bodies as a living sacrifice: "Therefore, I urge you, brothers and sisters, in view of God's mercy, to offer your bodies as a living sacrifice, holy and pleasing to God—this is your true and proper worship," Romans 12:1 (NIV).

Experience the true worship of God
Applaud God all the times
Morning as often as you can
Evening as loud as you can
Celebrate God every worship day for He deserves
to be praised and glorified!

After all, according to Ephesians 5:20 (NIV): "always give thanks to God the Father for everything, in the name of our Lord Jesus Christ."

In the end, we must worship and praise
the King of kings for He is the Creator,
He is worthy, He is eternal, the Most High
and the only One
"from whom all blessings flow!"

"And you shall be holy to me for I, the LORD, am holy ..." Leviticus 20:26 (NKJV).We need to be like God for He is holy, gracious, and merciful.

"There is holiness when we relieve suffering, visit the sick, and comfort the bereaved. There is holiness when we love and serve – without any thought of reward or hope of personal gain. There is holiness when we love our neighbor as ourselves." Meyer Leifer Rabbi

2

Revelation from the Lord

"Yet a time is coming and has now come when the true worshipers will worship the Father in the spirit and in truth, for they are the kind of worshipers the Father seeks. God is spirit, and his worshipers must worship in the Spirit and in truth," John 4:23,24 (NIV).

The Lord appeared to me and joyfully
my eyes welled with tears –
For worship matters, indeed!

But I trust in your unfailing love;
my heart rejoices in your salvation.
I will sing the LORD's praise,
for he has been good to me,
Psalm 13:5,6 (NIV).

I saw a human form hidden behind the title
"Through Worship Only"
but I could not tell what it was.

The true worshipper must worship the
King with respect and fear!

I enter to praise who was and who is
and who is to come for in His presence
I find strength, security, and peace.
"For the Lord is near all who call on Him
who call on Him in truth!"
Psalm 145:18 (NIV)

It is not an easy thing to be confronted with a message from Father God, espccially when the message is not anticipated. But I also realize that as Apostle Paul beautifully puts it, "God has mercy on whom he wants to have mercy, and he hardens whom he wants to harden" Romans 9:18 (NIV). I humbly recognize that the Lord appeared to me in the past and more recently on Friday, November 14, 2014, in the early morning while I was still in bed asleep. I had a vision that I was walking on Flatbush Avenue in Brooklyn, New York in plain daylight. Unexpectedly, I observed the sun turns dark; it was then completely dark before a bright scripture light from heaven flashed up in the skies. All of a sudden, it was like a bright sunny day. I fell to the ground on my knees and read the sign in heaven that lit up the sky, it was so huge, so shiny, so marvelous, so beautifully written like a 3D font but superbly much better than a 3D font. It was a solid font, bright and bold with a human form behind the text.

I saw in the night vision, and behold, someone like a human form that I can hardly describe. His countenance was very bright like the Sun. But to me it was an angel of God or Jesus. His appearance was extremely lucent. The lighted scripture reads a well-written, brilliant message as sunlight "***Through Worship Only.***" My heart burst out with joy, and my first reaction was to kneel down on the sidewalk with both of my arms opened wide into the air, giving glory to God, thinking that Jesus is back. Suddenly, I started to cry loudly and joyfully: glory to God, praise the Lord and I started to weep until my face was covered with tears. My heart was racing like never before and it was filled with contentment and my tongue with praises. I was overjoyed. However, I noticed the other people who were on the street kept walking, minding their own business and I couldn't understand why they didn't stop to contemplate what I saw because it was so huge. The sign and the horizon were very bright. So huge and so bright that no one could miss something big like that. It was a moment of joy and celebration and I thought everything was just over. Suddenly I jumped from my bed. I woke up but it wasn't so and I was in shock. And I cried more, more, more.

Horrified in the presence of the Lord, I wondered "why me Lord?" because I do not deserve to see you. I was crying tears of joy, certainly because the Lord appeared to me from far away. I thought the trumpet was going to resound and Jesus was about to descend on earth. And I did exactly what I would normally do if I was awake. I knelt down and opened my arms widely to give praise to my God for He is so great toward a sinner like me. I was very terrified for my eyes to have seen the glory of my Savior.

After I jumped out of the bed, and fell on the floor, kneeling, and crying. My spouse was worried and asked what happened but I couldn't respond for I was in shock. I was astonished. I was very terrified for my eyes have seen the glory of my Savior. It was very difficult for me and very frightening, too. Indeed, it is not easy to be confronted with a message from heaven. I was amazed to be lavished with such favor and honor. I am a sinner and more tears came out and I kept saying thanks to God for pitying me with such a personal and powerful revelation. It is a great encouragement to me because I always take seriously my commitment to exalt my Savior but I was deeply shaken.

That is why I always love God because we read in Acts 10:34,35 (NIV): "Then Peter began to speak: I now realize how true it is that God does not show favoritism, but accepts from every nation the one who fears him and does what is right."

The mighty Lord satisfies me with the finest of the wheat

just like He satisfies His lowly servants. Later on I realized that it was very sweet to feel the presence of God this way. And Father God brought total peace in my heart. May my lips overflow with praise and thanksgiving for His mercy and His amazing grace to a sinner like me and to all wicked sinners!

Amazingly, Father God is a God of grace for He is mysterious, incomprehensible, and His grace is just sufficient for anyone who believes in Him and trust His words as the Apostle Paul wrote in 2 Corinthians 12:10 (NIV): "That is why, for Christ's sake, I delight in weaknesses, in insults, in hardships, in persecutions, in tribulations. For when I am weak, then I am strong." Later on that day, I sat down alone in the bedroom and let the peacefulness of the dream wrap around me. Suddenly, I started to think about the times when death came close to me in the past. On October 9, 2009, on my way to church, I was nearly killed on Jackie Robinson highway on the border of Brooklyn and Queens, New York. I couldn't explain or understand why I am still alive. An unbelievable miracle. More recently, on July 5th, 2015, on my way to visit a new born in Christ after a baptism, I parked my car and I came out cautiously due to oncoming traffic. Then approaching was another speeding vehicle that came to hit the driver door of my car and left me standing safely right by the door without seeing what exactly happened. I didn't see an angel or hearing a voice. I just know deeply in my heart that it was a blessing. I sensed that I wasn't alone and I couldn't stop saying that my Lord has a purpose for my life.

Today, I am insanely blessed to be alive. I definitely believe that God is with me despite my sinful character. Indeed, His gracious hand was upon me. As King David, I sat and asked: "Who *am* I, *Sovereign Lord*, and what is my family, that you have brought me this far?" 2 Samuel 7:18 (NIV). As Father God says to Moses in Exodus 33:19 (NIV): "I will have mercy on whom I will have mercy, and I will have compassion on whom I will have compassion." Besides, the book of Acts 2:17 (NIV) states clearly: "In the last days, God says, I will pour out my Spirit on all people. Your sons and daughters will prophesy, your young men will see visions, your old men will dream dreams." Regardless, Father God must be praised in the morning, at noon, and in the evening. As I prayed, I started to struggle with some questions: what I have done to deserve this vision? Why me for such a message about worship? Indeed, it is difficult to carry such a load.

I wrote this book because I believe there is a need to share this great manifestation with others for true worship is very important to Father God. The Almighty God deserves and is entitled to our worship. It was His intention in the beginning for us to worship Him constantly. In fact, according to Prophet Isaiah 43:7(NIV), *everyone who is called by My name, whom I created for My glory, whom I have formed and made."* Magister Dixit. So our sole life purpose is to worship Him. For that reason the enemy Satan stole the show from Father God, the Creator because he wanted to be worshipped instead. In fact, we were created to worship the Creator and to reveal His character daily.

No nonsense worship.

True and false worship

Compelling truth.org is presenting the truth about worship this way: "Worship is a life response to the worthiness of its object. When we worship God, we do so in response to who He is Psalm 52:9 (NIV). Our attitudes and actions reflect that we believe the character and conduct of God to be worthy of praise and adoration. At times our worship is expressed through corporate singing, teaching, and tithing. It is also expressed in our daily lives through prayer, Scripture reading, acts of kindness, gratitude, pure thoughts, and the like. We worship something when we act as if it has value. By nature, human beings are worshippers. Sometimes our worship is focused on that which is actually worthy of reverence (like God). Other times it is misdirected (for instance, we worship Hollywood, basketball or football stars and the like, our work, bank accounts, fashion or a political icon). Wherefore, we need to look at what it is to worship in spirit and in truth. It is important to note that we do this simultaneously. We do not worship in spirit in one setting and in truth in another. We are in both at once."

Indeed, true worship is a daily interaction with the Lord and one another; just like in physics: "the transfer of energy between elementary particles, between a particle and a field, or between fields." Remember, we are slaves to whatever masters us. Therefore, we cannot serve two masters and Jesus says it clearly: "No one can serve two masters. Either you will hate the one and love the other, or you will be devoted to the one and despise the other. You cannot serve both God and money" Matthew 6:24 (NIV).

Heart, mind, soul, and strength

Worshipping God involves all the above and it is so true that we must admit it involves all that we are. Father God wants all of us, not just part of ourselves but the whole being, which includes heart, mind, soul, and strength.

Seek His words and His presence.

Listen to His words.

Trust His words.

Love His words—implying to love Him and love all His children, the great law of Christianity.

Speak His words.

Act on His words.

Change the way we live—implying to change behavior towards other people.

Please Him with all of our being in all we do. Then in response we can worship His majesty for who He is, what He has done, what He is doing now, what He will do in the future, what He is worth, and what He has revealed Himself to be: a Father God of infinite possibilities. And only then can we praise His great name in spirit and in truth. And the proper attitude, the proper response is worship, which includes, of course, repentance, love, forgiveness, thankfulness, gratefulness, and joy.

Praise Him with words from our lips. Joyfully, come and let's adore the God of all creation. Come and read what I witnessed in the sky. It was a great manifestation. The glory of the heaven is indescribable. In fact, my language is too feeble to describe the vision. Indeed, what I witnessed in the sky was a great manifestation of the holy God. Father God has done great things for me and I praise my dear Lord for remembering not the sins of my youth. I thank Him for His favor upon me. For I trust Him and He is always my hope. "Throughout the world all systems of religion are losing their hold on mind and soul." So help me, Holy Ghost!

He will make all things new again

What is Jesus doing up there right now? We as His disciples, what should we be doing down here? Until that day when Jesus calls us

(His disciples) home, He is busy preparing many mansions for us. He is in a mission to make all things new. He is fixing everything broken. Until that day He is interceding for you and for me as He promised to all His disciples before going to heaven. As church leaders and disciples we are bound to follow His path. Bound to be faithful, obedient to His will. Bound to be humble. Bound to forgive one another.

Bound to be patient. Bound to love one another. And all those that who are faithful to His commandments. Those who are worshipping Him in spirit and in truth on a daily basis. Those who are willing to suffer. Those who bring the truth into practical life. Those who profess the truth, and have faith in the truth; those who are kind and sincere, those who are patient and those who are faithful and those who are a blessing for others—verily they are truly a great blessing to the world —they are called the righteous by the book of Proverbs. Those who claim they are serving God or make such profession as Christians and do not in fact reveal Christ in their works are just a curse to the world—they are called the fools, which is a sharp distinction. However, sometimes some of those we called fools are not really fools because we have been deceived so many times by those we once thought were wise and righteous. We are not supposed to be the judge at least for now; however, the righteous lives are the evidence of their faithfulness. "By their fruit you will recognize them," says, the Master, Matthew 7:16 (NIV).

Let God be the judge and we need to ask Him for such virtues like patience, kindness, love, forgiveness, sincerity, compassion, mercy, and wisdom. "For wisdom is the principal thing," Proverbs 4:7 (NKJV). Speaking about wisdom, don't you wonder why today we have more knowledge and less wisdom—less wisdom is unfaithfulness. What possible good can arise from less wisdom?

Only sin, misery, and suffering. So less wisdom is not worship in spirit and in truth!

Faithfulness to God

In seeking to live in faithfulness to God, one needs to be wise or have the fear of God because the wise are cautious in sorting out the good from the bad. They are humble. They are not self-assured. They enjoy the experience of learning and growing. They are compassionate and sensitive to others' needs; it is a great expression of faith when treating others as we like to be treated. They are calm and patient. They are dependent on God's help and they have great confidence in Father God.

In the worshipping assembly, the unfaithful fall away from the living and loving God. However, in His compassion the Almighty remains faithful and stands by his promise, even when His people are *unfaithful*.

In *Worship in the letter to the Hebrews*, Professor John Paul Heil writes, "The unfaithfulness of having an evil heart is further explained by its dire consequence, namely, 'in falling away from the living God' Hebrews 3:12 (NIV). To fall away from the living God would mean for the audience not to enter into God's own heavenly "rest" Hebrews 3:11 (NIV), the heavenly glory Hebrews 2:10 (NIV) and the heavenly world where God and His Son are worshipped Hebrews 1:6 (NIV)."

Therefore, to avoid *falling away*, we must persevere in *God's* truth with thankfulness and gratefulness. Undoubtedly, all things created are an expression of God's incredible power. Besides, everything He created is very good. His creativity is embedded with wisdom, love, and goodness and they revealed the glories of His divine character. All is for our benefit and for our happiness.

Indeed, I am truly amazed and joyful that the God of creation is still in the field of working wonders. All children of God are called out from the world to gather for true worship and fellowship!

"And what does the LORD require of you? To act justly and to love mercy and to walk humbly with your God," Micah 6:8 (NIV).

In the end, isn't it worship in the way we live, work, talk, play, and doing our everyday business?

After all, isn't our body the temple of the Holy Spirit of God. It should be offered "as a living sacrifice" daily!

My vision of the great and bright light from heaven is not just a coincidence when the book of *Selected Messages, Volume 3, P.387* clearly states the following: "America, where the greatest light from heaven has been shinning upon the people, can become the place of greatest peril and darkness because the people do not continue to practice the truth and walk in light."

Father God gave me a powerful revelation about worship, not because I have any wisdom whatsoever. It is not by my own godliness, it is God's grace to little me. Humbly, I am grateful to Father God and the ministry that He has entrusted me. This revelation will help many to worship in spirit and in truth. To Father God be all glory and praise for I don't deserve to see the holy Almighty God because I am vile – A sinner. A doubter like Gedeon, "Alas, Sovereign LORD!"

3

The insights of worship according to the book of Isaiah

The Three Angels

"Then I saw another angel flying in midair, and he had the eternal gospel to proclaim to those who live on the earth—to every nation, tribe, language and people. He said in a loud voice, Fear God and give him glory, because the hour of his judgment has come. **Worship him who made the heavens, the earth, the sea and the springs of water**" Revelation 14: 6, 7 (NIV).

Worship

every day is very important because we read in Lamentations 3:23 (NIV): "God mercies are new every morning; Great is Your faithfulness." So He deserves to be worshiped each morning. Pastor Jack Hayford added that "Worship changes the worshipper into the image of the One worshipped."

Worship is so important that we need to worship the Bright Morning Star whenever the moment, whether in a calm, quiet, chaotic moment, or during rough times.

Worship is so important that in Matthew 4:9 (NLT), the Devil said, "All this I will give you, he said, if you kneel down and worship me," but Jesus said, "*No.*"

And are you worshipping God or the Devil? Worship is not to be treated with neither indifference nor carelessness. It is sacred and not a show business where everyone comes to show off talents or self. In his book: *Worship matters: Declaring God's worth,* Dr. Mansfield Edwards puts it this way, "Just the singing of hymns and the scripture reading are not worship." The need for preparation is very important. The same way we need to start Sabbath preparation on the first day of the week, worship must be prepared during the week. Our spiritual preparation is an urgent need.

Spiritual preparation before worship day is the best way to guarantee true worship on the day of worship. A love relationship with one another is the prelude to worship.

Unfortunately, many of us think that we are worshipping God but we are really worshipping Satan. We are not worshipping in spirit and truth. This is because we adore Him with a tongue full of malice, clishmaclaver, and hatred as King David said in Psalm 5:9 (NIV): "Not a word from their mouth can be trusted; their heart is filled with malice. Their throat is an open grave; with their tongues they tell lies."

Are you loving and worshipping today?

If we can just trust and obey the Creator the world would have been so different and we all would be happy today, tomorrow, and beyond. In 2 Chronicles 2:20 (NIV) we read: "After consulting the people, Jehoshaphat appointed men to sing to the LORD and to praise Him for the splendor of His holiness as they went out at the head of the army, saying: Give thanks to the Highest for his love endures forever."

Our loving Father God deserves to be exalted, through songs, praises, and reflection.

True Fasting

When we worship our way and not God's way we adore Him in vain. In vain you sing, pray, and all your offerings are rejected by Father God because you fail to worship Him properly. You pray, pray, and pray and God seems to be distant. He is not answering the way you thought He would. Too much antagonism, a wicked tongue, or bitter conflicts are the real reason Father God turns His back. "There are six things that the **Lord** hates, seven that are an **abomination** to him: haughty eyes, a lying tongue, and hands that shed innocent blood, a heart that devises wicked plans, feet that make haste to run to evil, a false witness who breathes out lies, and one who sows **discord** among brothers" Proverbs 6 (NIV).

Worship Him with a sincere heart and He will do marvelous things for you.

"Shout it aloud, do not hold back. Raise your voice like a trumpet. Declare to my people their rebellion and to the descendants of Jacob their sins. For day after day they seek me out; they seem eager to know my ways, as if they were a nation that does what is right and has not forsaken the commands of its God. They ask me for just decisions and seem eager for God to come near them. 'Why have we fasted,' they say, 'and you have not seen it? Why have we humbled ourselves, and you have not noticed?'" Isaiah 58:1-3 (NIV).

The Lord continues: "Yet on the day of your fasting, you do as you please and exploit all your workers. Your fasting ends in quarreling and strife, and in striking each other with wicked fists. You cannot fast as you do today and expect your voice to be heard on high. Is this the kind of fast I have chosen, only a day for people to humble themselves? Is it only for bowing one's head like a reed and for lying in sack cloth and ashes? Is that what you call a fast, a day acceptable to the LORD? Is not this the kind of fasting I have chosen: to lose the chains of injustice and untie the cords of the yoke, to set the oppressed free and break every yoke? Is it not to share your food with the hungry and to provide the poor wanderer with shelter—when you see the naked, to clothe them, and not to turn away from your own flesh and blood?" Isaiah 58:4-7(NIV).

He further added: "Then your light will break forth like the dawn, and your healing will quickly appear; then your righteousness will go before you, and the glory of the LORD will be your rear guard. Then you will call, and the LORD will answer; you will cry for help, and he will say: Here am I, If you do away with the yoke of oppression, with the pointing finger and malicious talk, and if you spend yourselves on behalf of the hungry and satisfy the needs of the oppressed, then your light will rise in the darkness, and your night will become like the noonday. The LORD will guide you always; he will satisfy your needs in a sun-scorched land and will strengthen your frame. You will be like a well-watered garden; like a spring whose waters never fail. Your people will rebuild the ancient ruins and will rise up the age-old foundations; you will be called Repairer of Broken Walls, Restorer of Streets with Dwellings. If you keep your feet from breaking the Sabbath and from doing as you please on my holy day, if you call the Sabbath a delight and the LORD's holy day honorable, and if you honor it by not going your own way and not doing as you please or speaking idle words, then you will find your joy in the LORD, and I will cause you to ride in triumph on the heights of the land and to feast on the inheritance of your father Jacob. For the mouth of the LORD has spoken," Isaiah 58: 8-14 (NIV).

Furthermore, the Book of Proverbs, chapter 25 clearly states: "If your enemy is hungry, give him food to eat; if he is thirsty, give him water to drink. In doing this, you will heap burning coals on his head, and the LORD will reward you."

A little love, and a little compassion, a little forgiveness, and willingness to meet other people's needs can be the greatest expression of faith in God. That's worship, too. Worship is celebrating God's marvelous works and rejoicing among brethren so we all can fully enjoy all blessings from God's true promises— not hatred among brethren, which is cursing. No wonder why Jesus made this comments in Matthew 5: "Therefore, if you are offering your gift at the altar and there remember that your brother or sister has something against you, leave your gift there in front of the altar. First go and be reconciled to them; then come and offer your gift."

That is the acceptance of worship by Father God. In addition, how dare can we be followers of Jesus Christ and hold grudges? For holding grudges against one another is unacceptable to Father God. That is worshipping Him in vain. "*In Vain* Do They *Worship* Me,*"* declares the Master, Mark 7:7 (NKJV).

We are rejecting the teachings of God for the doctrines of Satan and his agents. We want other people to worship us just like Satan wishes. That is Satan's wishes for all of us. In reality we worship the enemy not Father God. Remember what Jesus told the Samaritan woman in John 4:24 (NIV). "God is spirit, and his worshippers must worship in the Spirit and truth."

Whether you worship publicly or privately we ought to worship enthusiastically, joyfully, and lovingly. We need to prepare ourselves to meet God during the week so on worship day when He is passing through you can receive your blessings. Do not let Him pass by you and do not let the world distract you or anything around you preventing you from receiving your blessings.

"Consider this, you who forget God, or I will tear you to pieces, with no one to rescue you," says the Lord, Psalm 50:22 (NIV).

He warns false worshipers. God expects true adoration, authenticable according to his word. As Apostle John states, "those who worship Him must do it out of their very being, their spirits, their true selves, in adoration," John 4:24 (MEV).

The theme song in Psalm 42 (NIV) says it right: "As the deer panteth for the water so my soul longeth after You.

You alone are my heart's desire, and I long to worship You.

You alone are my strength, my shield, to You alone may my spirit yield. You alone are my heart's desire, and I long to worship You."

Healthy body VS Healthy mind

If the body needs proper diet, good balance, and good physical exercise, so does the mind. If the brain has a good healthy diet and good habits, the mind will be healthy. Neither distrust nor bad or negative thoughts should possess the mind. The enemy delights to see us mistrust God, our Creator. He enjoys toying with our minds in the same manner he did with Adam and Eve by injecting doubt, evil, hatred, perplexity, and disbelief in our minds then our imagination fills with false ideas against Father God. In fact, our hearts allow the mind to plant the seeds of discouragement, despair, and misery. Once your mind is under his control, the body is also affected with disease and the last result is physical and eternal death. He is exultant when he can make our life miserable and torture our minds with evil spirits, and doubt—creating a deep-seated distrust of a forgiving and loving God. We ought not to trust in our feelings but in God, the great Creator.

Imagination

Not too many people think that it is a duty for them to exercise some kind of control over their thoughts—over their imagination. Our thoughts need to be disciplined so Satan does not take over control. He knows that the mind is a very important part of us. He has many ways to take over control of our mind and prevent us from focusing on our worship: emotionally, sentimentally, food, diet, habits, superstition, indolence, pride, comfort, reliance on self, security in health, etc. We need to balance our desires and the passions that are brewing in us constantly. We need to be guarded by Jesus against the dangers of pride—the first sin committed in heaven. We need to watch our tongues, our lips, and our actions. That is worship. Doing good and overcoming evil with good is emulating the character of Christ. That is worship. That explains why "he who endures to the end shall be saved." Matthew 24:13 (NKJV). Enduring faithfully is very valuable for all worshippers.

Trust in God

We ought not to trust our feelings when worshipping the Creator. We need to trust our faithful Savior. All our afflicted souls should trust in His love. He loves us very much and He is trustworthy. Due to our sinful nature our mind is weak. And the narrowness of it makes it very difficult to comprehend God.

Make no mistake we have no reason to mistrust or doubt God's word even though He allows us to doubt. He can change the current state of our wicked minds and our thoughts for a complete transformation. Remember Satan came down from heaven with great power seeking to enter into our minds and hold us captive. Unless we surrender ourselves completely to Jesus, the only Savior, we are going to be the next victims after Eve. Having said that, should we not encourage the enemy to enter into our minds and take over control? For that when we feel that the enemy is trying to torture our mind with doubt we need to ask the Lord to come quickly to help us because our evil mind is so weak and so vulnerable that we need to have Jesus 24/7! Not just in emergency circumstances, for example, when dialing 911 in the United States of America for help.

You need to be certain when you come to worship God that your mind is in tune with His mind and you will be blessed so you can bless others.

King David was a worshipper for he wanted to live in God's House all the time. "One thing I ask from the LORD, this only do I seek: that I may dwell in the house of the LORD all the day of my life, to gaze on the beauty of the LORD and to seek him in his temple," Psalm 27:4 (NIV).

David worshipped father God actively, obediently, repentantly, enthusiastically, defensively, joyfully, and lovingly. In addition, he worshipped Him righteously, publicly, encouragingly, lavishly, repeatedly, melodiously, inwardly, and quietly. Like king David, live to worship Lord and praising Him in your bedroom – your living room – your kitchen – your bathroom – your car – your job – your farm – your school – and your office. A life of praise!

Applaud God loudly and often.

Baruch Hashem Adonai!

Blessed be the name of the Lord!

He deserves to be exalted, be worshipped and be praised. We ought to live to worship the Lord in this world so we can live in His kingdom forever!

4

You shall love your God with all your mind

I enter in your presence Holy God to seek
shelter for that it is where I belong!

Oh! Worship and praise the King
of kings in spirit and truth!

Through Worship Only.

as it was brightly and beautifully written in the sky. It also happens to be the title of this book as I saw it in my dream. It is not a man-made title. It is the Holy God's message to little me. A message that I gladly share with each and every one of you.

The book of Revelation is filled with prophecies, symbols, and figures about the future. In fact, many including the devil talk about the end of time and the return of Jesus. And the devil is racing to do as much harm as possible to a great many. Revelation 14:6-11 (NIV) announces the three angels flying from heaven with messages from God.

The first angel shouts loudly to all inhabitants of the Earth: "Respect God and worship Him. The time has come to judge who has been faithful and who has not." And in case there is confusion or misunderstanding about the true God, the angel added: "worship the Creator, the One who made the heavens and the Earth, the sea and the springs of water." And then the second angel shouts loudly, "Babylon is fallen!" What is Babylon? It is a place where false religion is born. Where the word of God has been twisted into a bunch of lies and leads many of God's children away from Him. And the third angel shouts: "anyone who worships the beast and his image and gets his 'mark' will feel God's wrath." Anyone who joins that group will receive the "mark" of the beast, contrary to those who refuse to join who will receive the "seal" of God.

The fall of Lucifer, Adam and Eve, and the alliance against heaven

Cleverly and craftily, Lucifer seduced many angels because he has two main purposes: usurp the throne of God and be worshipped himself. I called this action (The first "coup d'État"). "That is exactly what Satan has done in heaven, and today again his agents are doing just that on earth. Lucifer wanted to be on God's throne, and he became jealous of His Creator. He wanted to supplant God because he was full of knowledge, power, and unsurpassed beauty. Lucifer is a creation, but the object of his desire was God's throne, and he wanted to take the Almighty's power by force." (*Jesus, The Great Healer*).

He wanted the Creator to worship him. "Therefore, if You will worship before me, all will be Yours." Luke 4:7 (NKJV), says Lucifer to Jesus. And Jesus answered and said to him in verse 8: "Get behind Me, Satan! For it is written, 'You shall worship the LORD your God, and Him only you shall serve.'"

His selfishness and arrogance were definitely ugly and evil. His action of enticing is pretty darn egoistic. He was too proud of himself. There come the great dangers. The serpent draws our first parents to sin and misery, which proved fatal to them and to us. And we, too, have fallen into it. Today he continues to lead many away from obedience to God. An irresistible temptation that was deadly. They lost all because they chose to listen to the Serpent, the great deceiver. They were not left without warning of the great danger. The same holds true for us when we were told not to set up our will against the holy will of Father God. Understand, the enemy sought the occasion to control Adam and Eve and our ancestors' minds and did the same to Jesus as well but failed. Satan expects the Son of God to worship Him. "All this I will give you," he said, "if you will bow down and worship me." Matthew 4:9 (NIV). Materialism surely corrupts the mind.

"Worship me," says Lucifer to Jesus.

Consequently, Adam and Eve were driven out from the beautiful garden where they had happy moments of being the king and queen of the newly created earth because they didn't heed the warning of Father God, the Creator. An amazing passage in the book of the Prophet Nehemiah 9:5, 29-31 (NIV) describing a powerful revelation of God's mercifulness and loving-kindness toward the people of Israel throughout the history. "And the Levites—Jeshua, Kadmiel, Bani, Hashabneiah, Sherebiah, Hodiah, Shebaniah and Pethahiah—said: Stand up and praise the LORD your God, who is from everlasting to everlasting, Lord, You warned them in order to turn them back to your law, but they became arrogant and disobeyed your commands. They sinned against your ordinances, of which you said, 'The person who obeys them will live by them.' Stubbornly they turned their backs on you, became stiff-necked and refused to listen. For many years you were patient with them. By your Spirit you warned them through your prophets. Yet they paid no attention, so you gave them into the hands of the neighboring peoples. But in your great mercy you did not put an end to them or abandon them, for you are a gracious and merciful God!"

Because time after time the people turn their back on God; however, each time He restored them and blessed them generously. Regardless, He remained faithful to His selected people, the nation of Israel and all those who worship Him. The danger of falling under the power of Lucifer is obvious because the world is swimming, day by day, in a river full of satanic delusions. Many will be seduced by the power of satanic delusions. They will be deceived for failing to worship God in spirit and in truth. "Satan well knows that all whom he can lead to neglect prayer and the searching of the Scriptures, will be overcome by his attacks. Therefore he invents every possible device to engross the mind." www.whiteestaste.org/books

For millenniums, the kingdom of darkness (evil spirits, demons) has been battling the kingdom of light (righteousness) and the final great conflict is about to end. But the finishing line is getting tougher and tougher. In the meantime, the fight for the mind is going on. Many are in fact trying very hard like Satan did to Adam and Eve, to control other people's minds. Today, there are many private as well as public companies that are doing just that to trap us so we may stay focused on their products through constant TV, radio, and Internet Commercials advertising.

In addition, many so-called friends are "frenemies" ("frenemies" are people in our lives who purport to be a friend but do some oddly enemy-like things to us on more than an occasional basis, and in a way that seems pretty predetermined to unsettle us). That is exactly what Satan did to Adam and Eve when he tried to be a good friend, or a good counselor. He manipulated them to gain advantage in an unfair manner. He unsettled them to death and that was predetermined. So if some of your friends are trying to control you and if deceitful companies use commercial advertising to control your behavior, you are in bad shape. If this is the case, your mind is in dangerous hands. Because when your mind is being control by others it is not in good hands.

Therefore, you can't worship the Creator in spirit and in truth.

By the way, commercial advertising in the United States is very lucrative because it works well and is designed to control our mind. In fact, Apostle Paul says it right: "Don't you know that when you offer yourselves to someone as obedient slaves, you are slaves of the one you obey--whether you are slaves to sin, which leads to death, or to obedience, which leads to righteousness?" Romans 6:16 (NIV). And according to Statista Dossier, Advertising spending in the United States was expected to increase by 4.9% to almost $ 400 billion (USD) in 2016, compared to $158.3b in 2011. Online video advertising expenditure in the United States in 2014 as well as a forecast for 2016 is outrageous. Magnaglobal, a marketing firm based in New York projected the spending reached 9.14 billion U.S. dollars in 2016. Television will continue collecting the largest part of the expenditure but online advertising is catching up and is projected to record the highest growth rate among all media at 16.6%. The global digital ad spend is expected to amount to more than 252 billion U.S. dollars by 2018. Today, the United States are the largest advertising market in the world and according to forecasts, it is also expected to top the list in 2019. All these are the snares of Satan to draw the minds of humankind from worshipping God to worshipping money or Mammon. So beware of the dangers of materialism. And don't be lovers of your own self. For the same strategies Satan used to lure Eve into sin and through the ages He does the same for us as well. Indeed, a job well done. The first Adam was faithless to his Creator. But the second Adam (the Lord from Heaven: Jesus, the Messiah) was faithful to His Father. He came on Earth to restore the lost Garden of Eden and to redeem His people. The one from dust could not do the job because he was faithless. Only the second Adam was faithful. It is all about faith. *"Get behind me, Satan!"* says Jesus to Peter. Remember the great conflict started in heaven because of the authority and worship he was seeking. That explains why many who are Satan's faithful worshippers on Earth have it all apparently. For worship belongs only to God. Worship is the Creator's exclusive right. Worship belongs to God and God alone. Those who have faith are justified in the name of the Lord Jesus Christ: "For we maintain that a man is justified by faith apart from observing the law," according to the Apostle Paul, in Romans 3:28; 4:9 (NIV).

Larry Hurtado, a New Testament scholar, historian of early Christianity and Emeritus Professor of New Testament Language, Literature and Theology at the University of Edinburgh, Scotland, writes the following on an essay of Nicholas Thomas (N.T.) Wright, a leading New Testament scholar and retired Anglican bishop wrote regarding Apostle Paul and the Faithfulness of God: "I found stimulating his emphasis that in Paul the 'justification' of believers is essentially God's eschatological judgment, extended now to those who put faith in Jesus' vindication expressed in God raising him from death and exalting him to heavenly glory."

A new mind

According to the Bible, Jesus came to give us a new mind. This new mind is a change of heart-transformation. It begins with change of heart change of thoughts. "A new heart and a new mind will I give to you," (GNT). Why did the Prophet mention "a new mind"? Simply put, our actual mind is corrupted. Many want to live in a society free of corruption but we forgot that we are the problem because we all are sinners and sin is corrupt. Today, many Christians allow the devil to deceive them and make sinning acceptable. We should never ever ignore God's standard of morality and make up our own as we go in life. This is bad. The Bible teaches us that God's standard isn't negotiable or optional as things we can do now because *everyone is doing them anyway.*

Needless to say, God still loves us no matter how big our sins are; in return, we should express our love to God by obeying His commandments. Loving God and loving others as He commanded. In fact, who can bring the change we need in our society? Corruption comes from our minds. It starts from the minds of people, and like cancer and just like sin spreads in the universe. None of us can bring change for a society free of corruption or free of sins but Jesus. Fortunately, Jesus already won the battle against sin and the perpetrator. So only the Creator can give us back a new mind, free of sin. Therefore, a new mind is in the works according to His promise.

Why do we need a new mind?

A new thought creates a new mind. And a new mind is abundant life. Remember Jesus promised His disciples an abundant life. Those who choose to live in His presence will have an abundant life—they will have a new mind. Our actual mind is corrupt by the devil. The enemy doesn't want you to have an abundant life, which is why he is trying everything today again to control your mind. In contrary to God's character, which is filled with love and kindness as we read in the book of Prophet Isaiah 63:7, (NKJV). "I will mention the loving-kindnesses of the Lord, and the praises of the Lord, according to all that the Lord hath bestowed on us...according to his mercies, and according to the multitude of his loving kindnesses"; Satan's character is *filled with every kind of wickedness,* selfish ambition, jealousy, hatred, murder, envy, greed, discord, division, etc. Honestly, in Psalm 28:3, (NIV), King David reflects in his prayer regarding some: "who speaks cordially with their neighbors but harbor malice in their hearts." How they can worship the Almighty in spirit and in truth?

That is why Apostle Paul in Romans 1:29-32 states that some who claimed that they are following Jesus but in fact: "…have become filled with every kind of wickedness, evil, greed, and depravity. They are full of envy, murder, strife, deceit and malice. They are gossips, slanderers, God-haters, insolent, arrogant and boastful; they invent ways of doing evil; they disobey their parents; they have no understanding, no fidelity, no love, no mercy. Although they know God's righteous decree that those who do such things deserve death, they not only continue to do these very things but also approve of those who practice them."

Today again, that same satanic mouth has dropped such doubting thoughts about God, the Creator, into people's suffering heart, hasn't it? Understand that lifting up the mind toward God is always an expression of our adoration of God. That explains why the fight to control the mind is an ongoing affair of the devil and his agents until the end. So Satan can receive the adoration that only Father God deserves. "You shall have no other gods before me you shall not make for yourself an image in the form of anything in heaven above or on the earth beneath or in the waters below. You shall not bow down to them or worship them; for I, the LORD your God, am a jealous God, punishing the children for the sin of the parents to the third and fourth generation of those who hate me, but showing love to a thousand generations of those who love me and keep my commandments," Exodus 20:3-6 (NIV).

Satan despises the source of life. Many of us despise our source of life when we disobey God's commands. We take His grace for granted and we abuse His mercy as well as the unmerited blessings Father God has bestowed upon us. The enemy did gather all the rebellious angels to make war against God, the Creator, to do all unimaginable evil to humankind.

His plan is to ruin man's physical, mental, and moral powers. This way he will have full control of all men and women. He also leads us with a perverted appetite to drink liquor, to do drugs without control, and under the influence men would be led to abuse one another and commit all types of crimes. Through greed and alcohol, Satan spreads hate, division, jealousy and made all nations on earth corrupt. His main goals are to prevent us from entering the heaven gate because he and his acolytes will never be able to enter the heaven gate.

The book of Proverbs clearly warned us from the enemy, deadly deceptions, because he cleverly used wine, alcohol, and tobacco as his favorite destructive weapons to destroy the human family. So he is doing all he possibly can to destroy us all. Before that he made sure that we adored him through his human agents. Today, abhorrent characters with no moral decency, especially in the entertainment and in the sports industries are contemplated by many of us. And they are adored.

They are idolized.

They are worshipped.

They are honored.

They are glorified.

They are exalted.

We idolize and worship them like we are supposed to do only for the Creator. It is a sin to adore and worship golden calf, gods of wood, cement, silver, gold, diamond, river, sea, humans, or things – isn't this idolatry? For we will not be blessed at the end.

Many of us are worshipping the sun, the moon, a particular star or a celebrity, a particular beast, the worship of nature or earth, a portrait of man-made god.

The Evidence Bible comments in Deuteronomy 28:47: "Because you served not the LORD your God with joyfulness and with gladness of heart... therefore shall you serve your enemies which God will send you in hunger, and in thirst, in nakedness, and in want of all things and he shall put a yoke of iron upon your neck until we have destroyed you."

Simply put, we failed to *Worship* the LORD in truth. Distressed, frustrated, and feeling overwhelmed because life denied you the opportunities that others are enjoying.

So why worship you asked?

Some believe life is not worth living. Life is meaningless. In fact, when in distress, in anguish, and in sorrow or discouraged with all the snares of life; turning to Jesus and worshipping Him is the appropriate attitude—an attitude of gratitude for life and the air we breathe every day and all the joy Jesus puts in our hearts. Indeed, gratitude inspires attitude. Another form of daily worship is found in the book of Proverbs, chapter 21 verse 3: "To do righteousness and justice is more acceptable to the Lord than sacrifice." (NKJV).

In these postmodern times, youth and young adults need to remember that serving the Lord and worshipping Him on a daily basis is the right approach and walking with Jesus is a sublime relationship of love, forgiveness, and sharing. That is when you experience happiness, joy, and peace—*through worship only.* They need to understand that the Bible is the only truth book. According to Psalm 36:9 *"For with you is the fountain of life; in your light we see light."* Do not let others control your mind until they consume you because their negative opinions do have power and can really destroy your mind. In the battlefield of the mind, only Jesus can spare yours because He is the Maker. Just give Him your mind's adoration and join in the battle of the truth!

The battle for your mind is on

The devil's task is to attack your mind like he did to Eve. So don't allow the devil to deceive you and make sinning acceptable. Many believe in a new kind of standard like God can change with time—as though with a new century, there is a "new standard", a free-life style with a new God. "For I am the Lord, I change not;" Malachi 3:6 (KJV).

Today, more than ever, our mind is under constant attack by the great deceiver of souls. Unless our mind is resting in the hands of Jesus we are deemed to perish both in this world and the world to come. Every effort must be made so our mind can remain focused positively because positive thinking is our only assurance that our mind is in good hands—in the hands of our Redeemer.

The last desperate effort of Satan to overcome the faithful is to continue spreading lies and deceptions to confuse and control the minds of men and women. Instead, dream of Jesus and believe in Him. Trusting Him with all our hearts is our only escape.

Satan has many snares to deceive us just like he deceived Eve, many years ago. He is a liar today just as he was yesterday. We need to watch out so we don't get hurt badly. And the only way to be safe is to be in Jesus, the great Conqueror of the Universe. The enemy knows obedience starts in the mind. Thus, the mind is to be kept pure and clear from Satan's illusion.

The greatest victory of all times

Sin is a terrible thing because it is powerful. Satan and his agents are doing their best to seduce us all so beware of the enemy attack. He can disguise himself as an angel of light and in doing so was his successful way of winning Adam and Eve's hearts. But glory to Father God He set us all free through the work of lowly Jesus.

Do you have place for worship in your heart?

In your heart, do you have a place for worship? Like the rich young man, he was happy to keep the commandments and attend church services and worship regularly and so on but he has no place for Jesus in his heart. He was not worshipped in spirit and in truth. The same is also true for a great majority of people.

The dangers of worshipping false gods

Today, worship Baal is common in this world like in the ancient times. In an article published by the *Biblestop.com*, the author explains: "Baal worship is alive and well in America and the world – though they do not call it that today. First we must look back in time, and see how Baal was worshiped. Actually, there were two gods, which were essentially worshiped the same way, Baal and Ashtoreth. Moloch was another such god. Two practices in particular are mentioned in Scripture. First were sexual orgies 'under every green tree,' where promiscuity and perverted sex acts were the norm. Second was passing their babies through the fire. This was murdering the babies that resulted from the orgies by throwing them alive into a fire pit to be burned to death.

These things were done in the name of the pagan idol-gods Baal, Ashtoreth, and Moloch. How are we doing this today? The gods have been renamed 'Sexual Freedom' and 'A Woman's Right to Choose.' The religion is called 'Pleasure and Convenience.' We live in an age of loose moral standards, where it is acceptable and encouraged for us to have sexual partners outside of marriage. Just watch television; there is hardly a show on TV that does not glorify hunting sexual partners, or having such relationships without being married first. Then when the seed bears fruit, we murder the unborn baby. One method of abortion is a saline/chemical solution injected into the womb, which literally burns the baby to death. Another is to go in with a knife and cut the baby up (torture and cutting also being a popular form of satanic worship). Then there is the partial birth abortion, where they crack open the skull of a partially born child and suck out the brain with a vacuum. The priests are the abortion doctors, and the teachers are our television writers/producers and others who promote this lifestyle. One of the high temples is 'Planned Parenthood,' an organization whose sole purpose is make modern Baal worship acceptable to the people. In ancient times much of Israel was drawn into Baal worship. Their neighboring countries practiced it, so they wanted to practice it too, to get along with their neighbors. God called them out to be separate, but they wanted to be liked by the world. History repeats itself. Many churches today take a soft stance on sin, particularly sexual sin as well as homosexuality. Divorce/remarriage and sexual immorality of almost every kind is found almost as often in many of our churches as it is in the world. Some even approve of abortions. Like the ancient Jews, they are mixing worship of Christ with worship of Baal." (Biblestop.com)

Those of you that still worship Baal of Peor today, now read this in Deuteronomy 4:3 (NIV) and beware: "You saw with your own eyes what the LORD did at Baal Peor, The LORD your God destroyed from among you everyone who followed the Baal of Peor."

Nowadays, many people have place in their hearts for enjoyment of pleasures not for worshipping the Creator. They are honoring movie stars, entertainment, and sport celebrities. And in many instances, they are more popular than God, the creator. They like spending time outdoors and supporting or honoring celebrities and when winter arrives they remain inside using their TV sets a lot more and continues to worship them. In fact, they have lots of things on their minds other than worshipping Father God anyway—usually immediate gratification and pleasure. Remember what the devil told Jesus in Matthew 4:9 (KJV): "And saith unto him, All those things I will give thee, if thou wilt fall down and worship me."

As Apostle Paul writes in his letter to the Romans 10:3 (KJV): "For they being ignorant of God's righteousness, and going about to establish their own righteousness, have not submitted themselves unto the righteousness of God."

Isn't it the same for many who claim to know and to follow Jesus? That is why we need to submit ourselves to God today. We need to hold on because the final conflict is about to end soon. In the end, what do you really get from not having your mind controlled by no one but Jesus, your Creator and your Redeemer? Honestly, we deserve to die but Christ took our punishment on Him. He took our guilt and declared you are innocent. Instead of receiving your due punishment—eternal death, instead you are receiving eternal life. Real life is not a zombie life—it is an abundant life on this Earth and in the world to come.

Worship the Lord of lords from heart to head to feet!

Thus, as the great controversy started over worship when Lucifer wanted to become higher than Father God, his Creator; and there was war in heaven over worship but Lucifer, the dragon didn't prevail: You said in your heart "I will ascend to the heavens; I will raise my throne above the stars of God; I will sit enthroned on the mount of assembly, on the utmost heights of Mount Zaphon. I will ascend above the tops of the clouds; I will make myself like the Most High," said Lucifer, in the book of Prophet Isaiah 14:13, 14 (NIV).

Therefore, the ultimate victory of Christ is the ultimate demise of Lucifer. And the end of the struggle—the great conflict that rages around us—is near.

So our final victory is *THROUGH WORSHIP ONLY.*

We ought to yield ourselves daily to Father God for daily supply of grace – daily spiritual preparation through prayer – daily surrender to the influence of the Holy Ghost – daily witnessing.

All is part of true worship!

5

Let Us Adore Him and Rejoice in Worship

I enter in your presence Holy God to seek
shelter for that is where I belong!

"God is spirit, and his worshippers must
worship in Spirit and Truth,"
John 4:24 (NIV).

"Stand up and praise the L<small>ORD</small> your God,
who is from everlasting to everlasting"
Nehemiah 29:5 (NIV).

O Come, adore God and worship Him in spirit and in truth forever and ever!

For He deserves to be worshipped,

Let us bow down in worship.

Let us bow down to our Maker.

Let us come with thanksgiving before Him so He is our God.

Let us come before Him with joyful songs and worship Him with gladness.

I submitted this book to all of my readers with humility, for apart from Father God I am nothing. This revelation or any other knowledge from God's word is in fact given only by His grace. It is only by His grace, for I don't deserve it. My hope is that this reading may change your entire life and your walk with Jesus as it does for me. Not that I am better than anyone else but because of His love. A powerful revelation is given by the Holy Spirit. My God revealed His love for me personally and the importance of worship.

Every creature, servants of God, as well as all created men have a critical role in the worship of Father God, the lone Creator of the Universe.

The rationale of worship is to acknowledge the presence of God. Although the early church worship is centered on praising God, it is very important both for us and Father God. In truth, isn't in worship we get the blessings. We need to worship the Bright Morning Star regardless of the moment—whether in a calm, quiet, chaotic, or rough times. Besides Deuteronomy, Psalm 100 (NIV) brings out and emphasizes the true meaning of verses 1, 2, 3, and 5 where we read: "Shout for joy to the LORD, all the earth. Worship the LORD with gladness; come before him with joyful songs. Know that the LORD is God. It is he who made us, and we are his. For the LORD is good and his love endures forever; his faithfulness continues through all generations."

That explains why we should be joyful in our worship. He wants us to be joyful in our worship and express it. If not, we need to find out the cause in our relationship with Him because there must be something standing between us and God. Furthermore, worship is obedience, faithfulness, trust, loyalty, acknowledgment which was the attitude of Abel towards Father God unlike his brother Cain. See Genesis 4:1-5.

Worship day

On worship day, all worshippers should not come with discouragement, sadness, or vengeance, but be full of Hope— believing and expecting the blessings of God's promise. Worship is not gathering for fun like a friendly social club; the sanctuary is strictly reserved for worship. It is a sacred place. To impress upon us the importance of worship, Apostle Paul insists to "let all church meetings be done for edification": "Let all things be done decently and in order," 1 Corinthians 14:26, 40 (NKJV).

Jesus Clears the Temple Courts

"When it was almost time for the Jewish Passover, Jesus went up to Jerusalem. In the temple courts he found people selling cattle, sheep, and doves, and others sitting at tables exchanging money. So he made a whip out of cords, and drove all from the temple courts, both sheep and cattle; he scattered the coins of the money changers and overturned their tables. To those who sold doves he said, get these out of here! Stop turning my Father's house into a market!" John 2:13-16 (NIV).

Isn't it time we stop throwing out what Father God says to push our own agendas? Thus, our worship is in vain!

Do you ever listen to people who push aside what God's Word teaches and push their own agenda? See what Jesus says to the Pharisees Mark 7:8: "You have let go of the commands of God and are holding on to humans traditions." Oftentimes, our attitude is no different than the Pharisees.

A sacred or common worship

To know that your worship is following God's pattern and that it is not in vain, in fact, we need to refer to His word. Because there is only one way you can know when you worship in true and in spirit: you must get into God's Word and read it for yourself and practice it every day! Gracefully, light from heaven regarding the issue of worship—what worship should be and how to worship—is revealed through the book of revelation. With assurance, we come to worship His majesty and to bless and to receive His blessings as well. And His true desire is to do just that because as Psalm 118:24 (ISV) puts it: "this is the day that the Lord has made. Let us rejoice and be glad in it."

Hope in His goodness, His compassion, His love, His power, His faithfulness refreshes the worshippers with courage during the difficult moments, or after a week of heavy laden. And the exercises of loving others come with assurance that your worship will not be in vain. Furthermore, in the judgment day we will answer to Father God for every careless word and every careless action.

We all witness that the concepts of *good* and *evil* are blurred when many challenge God's word with their false interpretations and still believe they will be accepted by God in the name of love and it is all right to do so. What an aberration! As if God is changing color every day. They failed to discern the sacred and the common. Lord of mercy!

"When Ezra the scribe stood on a high wooden platform built for the occasion... [today we might call it a pulpit] Ezra opened the book [the Law of Moses]. All the people could see him because he was standing above them; and as he opened it, the people all stood up. Ezra praised the Lord, the great God; and all the people lifted their hands and responded, 'Amen! Amen!' Then they bowed down and *worshipped* the LORD with their faces to the ground" (Nehemiah 8:4-6 (NIV).

A genuine response

As the Psalmist praise Him in Psalm 150 (KJV): "Praise the Lord. Praise God in his sanctuary; praise him in his mighty heavens. Praise him for his acts of power; praise him for his surpassing greatness. Praise him with the sounding of the trumpet, praise him with the harp and lyre, praise him with tambourine and dancing, praise him with the strings and flute, praise him with the clash of cymbals, praise him with resounding cymbals. Let everything that has breathed praise the Lord."

We need to be respectful and reverent before Father God because He is perfect, holy, just, loving, powerful, and righteous. We cannot play with a sacred personage like God even though we cannot see Him and that explains His holiness for we are sinners and wicked. And because of whom He is. Adoration is a reverent honor paid to Father God, a sacred personage. No wonder why He asked us in Exodus 20 (NIV) to honor our father and mother.

For He deserves more than the honor we give to our earthly father and mother. One cannot argue that we all need to worship the good Lord who loves us so much and above all unconditional love forever. We should rejoice for His faithfulness and His immutable love forever. For He is the King of kings and Lord of lords forever and ever! Abel worship was a genuine response – an obedient one to God's word. And you? What your response should be! "To obey is better than sacrifice," 1 Samuel 15:22 (NIV).

Eternal worship on the new earth

What the new earth will be like?

The new earth will be where the tabernacle of God will be with the saved humans. The new earth will be real because God is real.

The new earth is where the lovely and the unlovely souls will meet at the intersection of forgiveness and compassion.

The new earth is where the Bright Morning Star wants to live with us and be our Friend forever in happiness.

The new earth is where we will worship the Holy God eternally.

The new earth is where the angels sing and worship the Creator.

The new earth is where God will dwell with His people.

The new earth is a place where the Bible mentioned some prophets of God like Elijah and Enoch were taken by God.

The new earth or the "New Jerusalem" is where all saints and martyred Christians will live with Jesus Christ.

The new earth will be a place of joy, happiness, and peace forever and ever.

The new earth will be here, because God is faithful.

The new earth is a place where loving-kindness will reach its climax, where we will see things we never seen or heard before for those who love others and God. However, as it is written: "What no eye has seen, what no ear has heard, and what no human mind has conceived—the things God has prepared for those who love him—these are the things God has revealed to us by His Spirit." 1 Corinthians 2:9,10 (NIV).

The new earth will be a place for love, peace, justice, and exhilaration only. Finally, the new earth, the kingdom, the city of Zion, the New Jerusalem, will be a place where the saints, the transformed, and the saved will share eternal life with Jesus, the Risen Savior. And the inhabitants shall not say: I am sick. The Bible says: all pain, all sorrow, all sickness, all crying, all death will be no more! Revelation 21:1-5.

O Worship the Lord in the beauty of holiness.

Bow down before Him, His glory proclaim;

With gold of obedience, and incense of lowliness,

Kneel and adore Him; the Lord is His name!

Remember this every day: "The heavens declare the glory of God; the skies proclaim the work of his hands," Psalm 19.

Shouldn't we do the same here, too? Every day!

Sanctuary and adoration

Thus, according to the Bible, "the heavens and the earth were completed in their entire vast array. By the seventh day God had finished the work he had been doing; so on the seventh day he rested from all his work. **Then God blessed the seventh day and made it holy**, because on it he rested from all the work of creating that he had done." Genesis 2:1-3. (NIV).

So far it is the only sanctified day in the Bible; it is **the only**

holy one the Creator has made for adoration, neither the first nor the second, the third, the fourth, the fifth or the sixth.

Having said that, why is there so much obstinacy and provocative conduct regarding worshipping the Creator on His **holy day**? When dealing with the Lord, is it always better to submit and surrender to Him with obedience instead of making things harder on ourselves. Let's take a look at the earthly sanctuary, which is a replica of the heavenly sanctuary. The Lord told Moses, "Let them make me a sanctuary; that I may dwell among them" (Exodus 25:8, NKIV). Keep in mind that this earthly tabernacle was never intended to be an edifice to shelter God from the elements. Jehovah is not a homeless God. When Solomon was building the first temple in Jerusalem, he said: "But will God indeed dwell with men on the earth? behold, the heaven and heaven of heavens cannot contain thee; how much less this house that I have builded?" (1 Kings 8:27, NKJV). Every component, from the largest curtain to the tiniest piece of furniture, had a symbolic meaning that helped the children of Israel see, experience, and comprehend the plan of salvation and the role of the heavenly sanctuary in a very practical way. (Biblia.com/bible/).

The acceptable worship

According to Prophet Isaiah, the Lord said: "I'm sick of your sacrifices. I'm sick of your sabbaths and holy days. I have no pleasure in the blood of bulls and lambs and goats... Stop bringing meaningless offerings! Your incense is detestable to me. New Moons, Sabbaths and convocations — I cannot bear your evil assemblies. Your New Moon festivals and your appointed feasts my soul hates...When you spread out your hands in prayer, I will hide my eyes from you; even if you offer many prayers, I will not listen." Isaiah 1:11-15 (NIV). See also, Jeremiah 9:6 (NKJV).

The people were doing rituals, bringing animals, keeping Sabbaths and festivals, even praying, but despite all that, there was something seriously *lacking* in their worship.

Why didn't God like their worship? He does *not* say they were keeping the wrong days or doing the rituals incorrectly. The problem was that their lives were full of sin. So in the first chapter of Isaiah, Prophet Isaiah counsels: "Your hands are full of blood; wash and make yourselves clean.... Stop doing wrong, learn to do right! Seek justice, encourage the oppressed. Defend the cause of the fatherless, plead the case of the widow" Isaiah 1:16,17 (NIV).

Their sacrifices, prayers and praises were not accompanied by performance in their day-to-day lives. They had worship rituals, but they did not obey God's commands for how to treat their neighbors, and the result was unacceptable worship. As Jesus said, quoting Isaiah 29:13 (NIV), "their worship was in vain. It was hypocritical to do the worship if it wasn't changing the other aspects of their lives."

For worship to be acceptable to God, we must have obedient lives. The ritual is not enough—the attitude is what is most important. God does not want hypocritical worship, or for people who say he is great but do not act like it. Perhaps this is commandment number 2 regarding worship—that it must be sincere. If we are going to say that God is worthy of all worship, then we should believe it in our hearts, and if we believe it, it will show in our everyday actions. True worship changes everything we do, because it changes who we are. Worship must be in the heart, not just at the place of worship. In final, true worship is an everyday affair.

Notice Jesus' own words in Matthew 25:34-36 (NKJV):

"'Come, you blessed of My Father, inherit the kingdom prepared for you from the foundation of the world: for I was hungry and you gave Me food; I was thirsty and you gave Me drink; I was a stranger and you took Me in; I was naked and you clothed Me; I was sick and you visited Me; I was in prison and you came to Me.'"

Here we go again, another aspect of true worship.

Oh! The Master and Savior desire only "mercy"!

So we ought to live and serve Father God, and be a blessing for others. This is true worship!

In the end, don't you feel the need to reject the devil and all his sneaky truths and lies – sneaky lies, oh; there are plenty the enemy wants us to believe. Wherefore let us be grateful and start worshipping the lowly Jesus in "spirit and truth" as He wishes?

6

The twenty-four elders in adoration

I enter the holy of holiness to praise
and worship the God of Abraham, Isaac,
and Israel because He is worthy!

The twenty four elders and the four living creatures said,
"Amen," and the elders fell down and worshipped who was
seated on the throne and they cried: "Amen, Hallelujah!"
Revelation 19:4 (NIV)

I enter to bless thee, the Lord of Hosts,
to exalt Elohim, and worship Adonai
for His name is Holy and there
is no one like Him!

Come,

Oh come all ye faithful to adore our great Lord with the Twenty Four Elders!

Worship of the Creator

And when the living creatures give glory and honor and thanks to Him who sits on the throne, to Him who lives forever and ever, the twenty-four elders will fall down before Him who sits on the throne, and will worship Him who lives forever and ever, and will cast their crowns before the throne, saying:

"Worthy is You, our Lord and our God, to receive glory and honor and power; for You created all things, and because of Your will they existed, and were created." Revelation 4:9-10 (NIV)!

Worship is for you, too

According to Wikipedia: Planning (also called forethought) "is the process of thinking about and organizing the activities required to achieve a desired goal. It involves the creation and maintenance of a plan, such as psychological aspects that require conceptual skills. There are even a couple of tests to measure someone's capability of planning well. As such, planning is a fundamental property of intelligent behavior."

Having said that, Father God has been planning even before the creation of all things, He knows that men will need a day of rest so they can come in His presence not just to worship Him because He deserves it, but we, too, need to be physically refreshed for the new coming week. Worshipping Him in spirit and truth brings pleasure and delight to God—but it also does something for you. King David knows very well that worship of Father God, the Creator of everything is beneficial to him as well. It is the reason we read in Psalm 84 (NIV):

> "Better is one day in your courts
> than a thousand elsewhere
> I would rather be a doorkeeper in the house of my God
> than dwell in the tents of the wicked."

As a great planner, Father God knew well in advance we will be robbed of our joy during the week, after six days of labor.

Did you know that worship isn't only for God? When you worship God, it brings pleasure and delight to God, but it also does something for you. There are benefits that come from being in God's presence through worship. Psalm 16:11 (KJV) tells us, "You reveal the path of life to me; in your presence is abundant joy; in your right hand are eternal pleasures." The psalmist says that worship brings joy. Being in God's presence lifts us up emotionally.

When joy has escaped you it is time to worship. When life has crushed in on you, it is time to worship. When the devil has robbed you of your happiness, it is time to worship. When Satan has surrounded you or circumstances have surrounded you with things that bring you down, it is time to worship.

The reason King David ran to worship is that he knew where the joy was—in God's presence is fullness of joy. So if you want to be lifted up in your spirit and emotions, go to God. Sing to God. Bless and thank Father God. Tell God you love Him. Cast all your anxiety on your Father, His comforts will satisfy your soul, according to His promise. You don't find joy by looking for joy. You find joy by being in an environment of joy. And believe me, God lives in an atmosphere of joy. You can't live in the atmosphere of the sun and not be hot. You can't live in the atmosphere of the cold and not get chilly. And you can't live in the atmosphere of God and not have joy. I recall many asked "why you always smiling and joyful?" It is because I have Jesus in my life, I replied.

O Come,

My dear reader, with thankfulness, joy, and gratefulness to worship Father God for His compassion. Let us come before him with thanksgiving and extol him with music and song.

"Let us come before him with thanksgiving and extol him with music and song. For the LORD is the great God, the great King above all gods. In his hand are the depths of the earth, and the mountain peaks belong to him. The sea is his, for he made it, and his hands formed the dry land. Come, let us bow down in worship, let us kneel before the LORD our Maker;"
Psalm 95:2-6 (NIV).

According to an article published recently
by David Mathis, we read:

"The issue is not whether we will worship, but what. Even better, *whom* and *how.*"
As many of us ready ourselves for corporate worship, perhaps the most significant single biblical text for guiding the essence of what we're pursuing together when we gather is Jesus's words in John 4:23,24 (NKJV):

"The hour is coming, and is now here, when the true worshipers will worship the Father in spirit and truth, for the Father is seeking such people to worship him. God is spirit, and those who worship him must worship in spirit and truth."

Heart and Head in True Worship

"True worship, says Jesus, is in *spirit* and *truth.* The "truth" part is plain enough—and with the coming of Jesus ("the hour is coming, and is now here") that truth centers on his person and work, the one who is himself "the Truth" John 14:6 (NIV) and the message about his saving accomplishments for us, which is "the word of the truth, the gospel" Colossians 1:5 (NIV) and "the word of truth, the gospel of your salvation" Ephesians 1:13 (NIV). It is this "word of truth" James 1:18 (NIV) by which we're given new birth, this "word of truth" 2 Timothy 2:15 (NIV) that Christian workers endeavor to handle, and this truth that anchors and saturates worship that is truly Christian."

God's servants or God's enemies

When worshipping, we need to come in the house of the Lord with a higher standard. We need to come humbly with a simple faith. We need to remember we are coming before His throne by grace not by proud boasts of perfection.

God's servants have no pride. The pride is gone with the wind. If it is not, when we come to worship, it is just like the people of Israel worshipping Baal, not the true God. We are worshipping our own god not the real God. Therefore, we are not *worshipping in spirit and truth.* We are God's enemies. Remember, we must give account to the Master. Let us be honest to ourselves. Real God's servants are faithful to His word.

At a time when the world is approaching its end, Satan is doing all he possibly can to steal the adoration from Father God. The enemy and his agents are fighting fiercely to convince us on a daily basis to turn our back on God. Unfortunately, many unfaithful worshippers cannot help but fail to worship the Almighty. When we fail to recognize that prayer and self-discipline are the most powerful weapons against the enemy, we fall short easily in the enemy's trap. As in the Garden of Eden, temptation, and illusion remain the best weapons of the enemy against the faithful God worshipers. Remember you come to worship and to give the Almighty thanks so He may fill your cup with joy in His presence!

Worship cannot be associated with anxiety. We need to admit that anxiety, anger, suffering, or being overwhelmed by trouble, sorrow, and sickness, can prevent us from worshipping God "in spirit and in truth." But if you cast off your anxiety, all your anger or all your sufferings on Him, he will take care of you!

I will worship You, Oh! Lord because you are great and worthy to be praised.

You are kind and wise to be blessed, dear Lord, you deserve to be exalted and glorified, you are compassionate to be magnified, you are worthy to be celebrated, and therefore we should worship our great Lord "*in spirit and truth*!" *Oh! Great is thy faithfulness!*

After reading this book, don't you think it is a great blessing to adore the Creator truly, to experience worship no more with negative emotions like sadness, hate, division, doubt, hostility, envy, worry, fear, frustration, jealousy, rage, and revenge?

On the contrary, we should worship with excitement, forgiveness, peace, patience, courage, grace, love, joy, faith, hope, confidence, happiness, assurance, sympathy, compassion, enthusiasm, positivity, contentment, thankfulness, and gratefulness to celebrate the Lord's Day in spirit and truth. "By the seventh day God had finished the work he had been doing; so on the seventh day he rested from all his work. Then God blessed the seventh day and made it holy, because on it he rested from all the work of creating that he had done," Genesis 2:1-3 (NIV).

Active participants or spectators

Sadly, there is a culture of spectatorship in the postmodern churches with a few exceptions. Many think that worship is entertainment. We ought not to become spectators neither observers for only the Creator is the spectator, no one else. We ought to be active participants in worshipping. Worship is where God talks to us and we respond to God. In some congregations where I have preached, I observed that in reading the word of God everyone sits still while we are supposed to stand up on our feet.

That is not right. We ought to stay up, praise, and sing. The same is true when worshipping in public; many shut their lips and fail to sing and praise God's wondrous works and His kindness. Jehovah El-Shaddai is the only spectator, not us. We are the participants.

Unfaithful worshipers are spectators not participants for they adore the Creator in vain.

Father: Forgive them the politics of spectatorship. If I could make one wish for them, it would be to make them worship your majesty in spirit and in truth.

Dear Lord, may everyone worship you sincerely in spirit and in truth, so I humbly pray!

As the author of Ephesians 1:3, 4 (NIV) declares:

"Praise be to the God and Father of Our Lord Jesus Christ, who has blessed us in the heavenly realms with every spiritual blessing in Christ. For He chose us in Him before the creation of the world to be holy and blameless in His sight."

Jesus is the only one who suffers terribly. He was given *His 300-pound cross* to *carry*. He bore the cross from Pilate's hall, and out of the city of *Jerusalem*, towards *Calvary* for approximately half a mile. At the time the soldiers forced Simon, the Cyrene to help Him.

Jesus has been tortured, humiliated, crucified, and died from asphyxiation.

Therefore, He is the only One who deserves to be glorified, praised, and worshipped. As is written in the gospel of Luke 4 (NIV): "The devil led him up to a high place and showed him the kingdoms of the world. And he said to him, I will give you all their authority and splendor; it has been given to me, and I can give it to anyone I want to."

"All this I will give you," Lucifer said to Jesus, *"if you will* bow down and *worship me."* Jesus answered: "It is written, worship the Lord your God and serve him only."

Oh! Come everyone to worship God Majesty happily, and celebrate joyfully His daily goodness!

Alleluia!

Dear reader, I would never write a book titled *"Through Worship Only"* but it is God's title not my own. This title enlightens the importance of worship for Father God and to impart knowledge to all worshippers.

I hope this book will enlighten all readers and bring hope, love, and encouragement, too. So we may not continue to honor the King of kings just with our lips but with our deeds as the first Christians did. "Worship the Lord in the splendor of his holiness; tremble before him, all the earth," Psalm 96:9 (NIV).

Today we all need a change in our minds as well as in our hearts. There must be a change in the way we act in the worship of the powerful Creator of heaven and earth.

May the good Lord be with you all until the time when we will meet in His kingdom for continuous worship!

A great sign appeared in heaven to me and it reads:

"THROUGH WORSHIP ONLY"

Worship Him.

Seek him who made the Pleiades and Orion, and turns deep darkness into the morning, and darkens the day into night; who calls for the waters of the sea and pours them out upon the surface of the earth: The Lord is his name, Amos 5:8 (NIV).

It is a very human inability to
imagine the unimaginable like
the act of worshipping Father God
in spirit and in truth!

"When Christ shall come
With shouts of acclamation
And take me home
What joy shall fill my heart
Then I shall bow
In humble adoration
And then proclaim
'My God, how great Thou art!'"
Stuart K. Hine

Conclusion

As we approach the end of time, like it or not, sooner or later humanity will have to face a decisive issue which is about worship. That is why we need to worship in spirit and in truth:

Whom are we worshipping today?

God, or the beast and its image.

We find the answer in Revelation 14:7 (NIV):

"The Angel said in a loud voice:

"Fear God and give Him glory, because the hour of His judgment has come. Worship Him who made the heavens, the earth, the sea and the springs of water."

Or do we adore the beast and its image?

If so, there is the warning we find in Revelation:14:9-12 (NIV):

"A third angel followed them and said in a loud voice: If anyone worships the beast and its image and receives its mark on their forehead or on their hand, they, too, will drink the wine of God's fury, which has been poured full strength into the cup of his wrath. They will be tormented with burning sulfur in the presence of the holy angels and of the Lamb. And the smoke of their torment will rise for ever and ever. There will be no rest day or night for those who worship the beast and its image, or for anyone who receives the mark of its name."

Whom are you obeying today?

God or the beast and its image?

This calls for patient endurance on the part of the people of God who keep His commands and remain faithful to Jesus.

The church of Christ demands obedience and faith. God's law is immutable. It is sacred and we are abiding by it. Those who are faithful to God will abide by His holy law, which is the Ten Commandments not 9 or 8 or 7 but the Ten Commandments. We just need to obey God's commandments. We have to comply if we really want to go to heaven, a real place. Walk, follow, and obey God's word daily so that we do not end up walking in the wrong direction, and following the wrong Savior.

Unfortunately, many of us do when we let religious beliefs, practices, and men tradition get in the way of doing what really matters to Father God.

Today God calls us as He called the angels who have become the heavenly partners to worship HIM.

Remain faithful until the end and be obedient to His word; this is what God asks all true worshippers!

Remain focused for we are almost home!

After all, life is not just for feel-good sensations packaged in adoration but true worship and glad adoration. I am sure this book on worship will aid you to experience peace and many blessings; however, only if you have a personal relationship with Jesus not an emergency one like dialing 911 in the United States of America for help!

And enjoy the rewards of worshipping and serving the Almighty God!

Cheer up, dear reader, make a joyful noise, sing a song, do what is right and just, and worship Father God in truth every day!

"Behold, He is coming with clouds, and every eye will see Him, they who pierced Him. And all the tribes of the earth will mourn because of Him. Even so, Amen."

Then the Master further added:

"I am the Alpha and the Omega, the Beginning and the End," says the Lord, "who is and who was and who is to come, the Almighty." Revelation 1:7,8 (NKJV).

The title of this book tells us
that it is
"THROUGH WORSHIP ONLY"!

I saw the Lord. I have fear.
I trust and obey Him. I worshipped my
Maker *"in spirit and in truth!"*

Let us adore Him and
rejoice in true worship every day!

Therefore, I urge you, brothers and sisters, in view
of God's mercy, to offer your bodies as a living
sacrifice, holy and pleasing to God—this
is your true and proper worship!
Romans 12:1, 2 (NIV)

After all, "even Jesus, the God of all creation as His custom was according to Luke 4:16 (NIV) attended the synagogue in Nazareth every sabbath day to worship"!

Thus, from dawn to dusk, The God of all
creation must be worshipped.
So be on your guard, worship your Creator.
For his court is in session!
"I long to dwell in your tent forever...!"
Psalm 61:4 (NIV)

Only be careful, and watch yourselves closely so that you do not forget the things your eyes have seen or let them fade from your heart as long as you live. Talk about them when you sit at home and when you walk along the road, when you lie down and when you get up,

Deuteronomy 4:9; 6:7 (NIV).

I, John, am the one who heard and saw these things. And when I had heard and seen them, I fell down to worship at the feet of the angel who had been showing them to me. But he said to me, "Don't do that! I am a fellow servant with you and with your fellow prophets and with all who keep the words of this scroll. **Worship God!**" Revelation 22:8,9 (NIV).

As the writings of Martin Luther helped bring about a mighty religious awakening in many countries; I do hope that "true worship" which had taken a back seat to human tradition regain its rightful place as the only way to meet Father God – *Through Worship Only*!

Endnote

Most of the Scripture quotations in this book are from the New International Version (NIV), Kings James Version (KJV), New King James Version (NKJV), New Living Translation (NLT), International Standard Version (ISV), Good News Translation (GNT), Modern English Version (MEV), and The Evidence Bible.

References

http://www.neverlosecontrol.com/

Nehemiah 9.

White, Ellen G., 2007, *Selected Messages, Volume3*, Hargestown, Review and Herald Publishing, 2007, P.387.

http://www.dictionary.com/browse/interaction?s=t

http://www.howcast.com/videos/393676-How-To-Spot-Frenemies.

www.jackhayford.org/teaching/articles/getting-to-the-heart-of-worship/

http://www.desiringgod.org/articles/worship-in-spirit-and-truth Advertising Market in the U.S. - Statista Dossier.

http://larryhurtado.wordpress.com/2014/03/17/paul-and-the-faithfulness-of-god-wrights-big-opus

http://www.gotquestions.org/theology-of-worship.html#ixzz3 Mux4RTJF

https://thebiblestop.wordpress.com/2012/01/10/baal-worship-is-alive-and-well-in-the-world/

www.stepintothestory.ca/tag/baal-worship

https://www.gci.org/God/worship

https://www.compellingtruth.org/true-worship-spirit-truth.html

https://thebiblestop.wordpress.com/2012/.../baal-worship-is-alive-and-well-in-the-world.

St. Louis, Ernst, (2013), *Jesus, The Great Healer,* Berrien Springs, Patterson Press publication, p.95.

Heil, John Paul, (2013), *1 Peter, 2 Peter, and Jude: Worship Matters,* Washington, D.C., Cascade Books.

Heil, John Paul, (2011), *Worship in the letter to the Hebrews,* Eugene, Cascade Books, P.61.

Holm, Jean, (1998), Worship, Emeryville, Alibris Publisher.

Mansfield, Edwards, (2013) *Worship matters: Declaring God's worth,* Ontario, Ontario Publishing, P.56.

www.wikipedia.com

https://en.wikipedia.org/wiki/Second_Temple

www.jewishvirtuallibrary.org/the-first-temple-solomon-s-temple

www.azquotes.com › Authors › R › Ralph Waldo Emerson

www.neverlosecontrol.com/specialoffer.php

https://en.wikipedia.org/w/index.php?search=pictue+of+baal
&title=Special:Search&profile=default&fulltext=1&searchToken
=9dkmffg88qpfgzo3lcn57ysn2

Above all, enjoy the rewards of worship
a marvelous Creator forever and ever!

Notes

Dyng To Save Others is both a spiritual journey into God's mission and the gift of eternity. Pastor Ernst St. Louis believes that loving God and loving others or even dying for them should be our only business. He shows eternal life to be an ever-deepening free-fall into friendship-love with God and His mission. This book provides the practical pointers to help everyone face the trials of carrying God's mission in this existence!

Jesus, The Great Healer stands ready to heal people's minds, spirits, and bodies. The healing power of love went out from Him to heal many diseases and ease the suffering of humanity. The great Surgeon can do the same for you, too. Indeed, He has the healing power. Just put your trust in Him. Pastor Ernst St. Louis shows Christ as a way to lasting health, peace and real joy for today, tomorrow, and beyond. *Jesus, the Great Healer*: "A detailed Bible," say many readers!

A must-read book for all

To send your comments to the author or for information on these books. Write to: comeditations@yahoo.com
Or call 1-917-940-1266